WALKING
IN THE
LIGHT

WALKING IN THE LIGHT

Basic Instructions for Every Believer in Christ

CARL V. MCCALMAN

iUniverse, Inc.
Bloomington

Walking in the Light
Basic Instructions for Every Believer in Christ

iUniverse books may be ordered through booksellers or by contacting:

iUniverse
1663 Liberty Drive
Bloomington, IN 47403
www.iuniverse.com
1-800-Authors (1-800-288-4677)

The views expressed in this work are solely those of the author and do not necessarily reflect the views of the publisher, and the author hereby claims all responsibilites for them.

Any people depicted in stock imagery provided by Thinkstock are models, and such images are being used for illustrative purposes only.
Certain stock imagery © Thinkstock.

All scriptures are taken from the King James Version of the Bible unless otherwise noted.

ISBN: 978-1-4759-4362-7 (sc)
ISBN: 978-1-4759-4363-4 (hc)
ISBN: 978-1-4759-4364-1 (ebk)

Library of Congress Control Number: 2012917094

Printed in the United States of America

iUniverse rev. date: 04/01/2013

DEDICATION

This book is dedicated to Apostle Irma Gimith Woerdings, the founder of Bribi (Faith) Ministries International, originating in Paramaribo, Suriname, South America. Apostle Irma is known as a woman of prayer who is devoted to interceding for ministries, nations, leaders, and peoples of the four continents to which she has traveled.

Some of the fruit of her ministry is seen in the more than twenty churches and scores of leaders she has raised up and in her anointing to lead the greatest fellowship in Suriname. It is a distinct honor to serve as a pastor in this great work that is touching the Caribbean, South America, Europe, Africa, the United States of America, and, by extension, the world. Her blessings, instruction, and guidance have proven to be beautiful signposts for me as I fulfill my commission from our Lord.

Author: Carl V. McCalman
Website: www.vivianmccalman.com
Phone: (347) 4421993

CONTENTS

Preface.. ix

Acknowledgments... xiii

Introduction xv

Chapter 1   A Born-Again Spirit Needs a New Menu ...1

Chapter 2   The New Birth Made Simple.......................7

Chapter 3   Water Baptism; What a Testimony!.........15

Chapter 4   The Local Church Is an Exciting
Place to Grow.....................................21

Chapter 5   Baptism in the Holy Spirit Is Glorious and
Powerful.......................................33

Chapter 6   Do Not Eat the Seed You Need to Plant...43

Chapter 7   Winning the Battle in the Mind 51

Chapter 8   Bumps in Our Path Can Strengthen
and Develop Us...59

Chapter 9   Experience the Joy of
Sharing Your Faith..............................65

Chapter 10 You're Not Alone, No, Never Alone 75

Chapter 11 Five Life-Transforming Prayers...............81
    i.   The Prayer of Repentance....................83
    ii. The Prayer of Intercession for a
        Lost Relative 84
    iii. The Prayer of Thanksgiving................86
    iv. The Prayer for the Healing of Sickness
        and Disease 87
    v. A Prayer for Divine Healing 90
    vi. The Prayer for Wisdom
        and Revelation.....................................91

Chapter 12 Meditations from the
              Psalms and Epistles...................................95
    i.   Psalm 27 97
    ii. Psalm 42 99
    iii. Ephesians 5:1-14 101
    iv. Colossians 3:1-13 103
    v. 1 John 4:1-11 104

The Power of the Blessing...109

PREFACE

I n November of 2002, my grandmother, Evelyn Sampson Thegg Austin, went to be with the Lord at the age of 106 years. At the time of her passing, she was a member of both the Congregational and the Methodist Churches. This was possible because she was a member of the Congregational Church when she married Mr. Austin; he was a minister of the Methodist Church. Evelyn loved to have her grandchildren around the things of God. I can remember awaking from a long sleep on the bench in the Congregational Church after what seemed to be a marathon meeting and rising early at home many Sunday mornings in order to have devotions that were primarily the singing of hymns and reciting of verses from the Bible.

God does not have grandchildren. My heart was bleeding one day as I sat on the steps of my grandmother's home. At the age of six, the reason for living and the meaning of life were overloading my mind. "What is the meaning of life?" I asked. "Am I like a dog or a cat that I have seen die and be forgotten?" I muttered. "Will I live for a little while, after which I'll die and be no more?" These questions haunted me. I wanted life to deliver more, and that desire set me on a journey. Along this journey, my path collided with God, and life's puzzles came together.

People quite often say they found God, but he was never lost. He found me at the age of twelve. At that time, early in 1971, I was living with my mother, a single parent, in Linden, Guyana, and next door was a little church. It held a gospel revival, and I stood before an old-fashioned altar, bowed my heart, and received the highest power: Jesus Christ, the Son of God. After that experience, I lived as a child of God for six months. Then I backslid, or left the faith, and returned to the Lord after approximately nine months.

For over four decades, I have lived as a Christian and served in various capacities of the local church. These include deacon, treasurer, Bible teacher, evangelist, and pastor. While serving in these positions, I have noticed many Christians fail and fall out of the faith. The big question is this: Why? Is the Christian life too difficult to live? I don't think so! In fact, I believe it is the best life anyone can experience. My conclusion is that the majority of Christians who failed were not properly established on the basic principles of the faith. Building your Christian life on God's principles will yield lifelong success. Proverbs 3:1-2 says, "My son, forget not my law; but let thine heart keep my commandments: For length of days, and long life, and peace, shall they add to thee."

For many years, the Lord placed a burden on my heart to make a statement that can help believers stay on his path for success. That statement is the purpose of this book. It introduces converts to the new life and gives clarity to the process whereby we turn from darkness to the light and continue to walk successfully in the rays of God's glory. True repentance is really switching to the light, who is Christ, and when we do, he will show us the new way. This book begins at that experience.

Everyone who seeks a solid foundation in the Christian faith will find these admonitions useful. Pastors, teachers, and lay preachers will find in it valuable tools when instructing new disciples as well as the older saints. The book will be a great help to evangelists both within and outside the four walls of the church. Indeed, it can be used for mass evangelism as well as personal witnessing (oh, how we need to teach personal evangelism in our churches). When a decision is made to receive Jesus, the seed of the word of salvation is fresh in the heart of this new believer. The information provided on these pages is meant to safeguard this fresh word so that the wicked one will not be able to stifle that which was sown (Matthew 13:19).

Yes, it is prepared to meet the need of new believers in Christ, but it will also help the older saints discover some areas they may have missed and offer them a clearer understanding of the new birth. In so doing, they will be able to correct mistakes they may have made and sharpen their skills in discipleship and personal witness.

Every chapter has doctrinal truths that can fill a thousand pages, but they have been condensed and simplified for every reader to comprehend. I have added beautiful examples of prayers every child of God should pray, as well as some of the most treasured, inspirational, and devotional scriptures from the Psalms and Epistles. The book ends with the power of the blessing. Please read joyfully, and every time you delve into the pages of this book, you will discover many ways to make the light of our Savior shine brighter through you.

ACKNOWLEDGMENTS

My heartfelt gratitude goes out to Brother David Elcock, a professional proofreader, retired broadcaster, and servant of the Lord, for his willing and dedicated assistance in reviewing the manuscript for this book. May God continue to bless him.

To sister Yvonne Ward and my niece Shenella McCalman who willingly offered their services to give this work the refined finish it needed.

In this book, you will find ten essential insights that will benefit you as you seek to be victorious in Christ by walking in the light.

INTRODUCTION

Welcome to the family of God! When you received Christ Jesus, our Lord, into your heart, you turned from darkness to the light. Ephesians 5:8 says, "For ye were sometimes darkness, but now are ye light in the Lord; walk as children of the light." It is truly a privilege to experience living as a child of the light, and darkness is the only other choice. What is darkness? The definition for this word can be very complex, but to say it simply, it represents the systems of the world and its peoples who are not in fellowship with God, his Son, and the Holy Spirit. This is a broad definition, but anyone can see the manifestation of darkness in his or her neighborhood on a micro level when a person engages in a despicable act or on a macro level, where its presence has engrossed many countries, religions, cultures, customs, and lifestyles of the world.

It is the operation of darkness that causes a man to assault and kill an innocent little girl. It was the power of darkness that inspired Adolf Hitler to ignite a blood bath in the Second World War, resulting in more than sixty-one million people (2.5 percent of the world's population) losing their lives and untold numbers injured. Paul, in writing to the church at Ephesus, says, "For ye were sometimes darkness but now are ye light in the Lord: Walk as children of the light."

John 1:4 says, "In Him was life, and the life was the light of men." Jesus gave to us his life, which shines, and we have become the light of the world. Each of us can receive this light on a personal level, and yet it is so powerful that its power has brought into existence great moves of God that have covered countries, nations, governments, and kingdoms. The saints and pilgrims left Europe in 1620 in search of the new world, the Americas, because they wanted religious freedom so that they could serve God the best they knew—that is, with all their heart. They formed the first colony—Plymouth colony—in Massachusetts and brought the Christian light to a dark continent. They had to struggle against many obstacles, but it was worth it. Every American can testify about that.

The founding fathers of this great country—George Washington, Benjamin Franklin, Alexander Hamilton, John Jay, James Madison, and Thomas Jefferson—were people who wanted the light of God to shine through them. They established the United States' Constitution on the Judeo-Christian principles of the Bible. This desire to give God's word preeminence gave birth to these United States, which is presently the most powerful nation on Earth and has been leading the world through great turmoil and economic failure.

We are commanded by God to walk as children of the light. This family connection became possible when we began our fellowship with Jesus, the Son of God. He is called the light of the world. Our newfound family relation with Christ should be valued dearly. Carelessness and lack of knowledge can cause unnecessary loss and failure to those who do not guard their experience with God.

In this book, you will find ten essential insights that will benefit you as you seek to be victorious in Christ by walking in the light. These insights are really intended to be the "appetizers" that will create a greater desire for more knowledge of this glorious life. Are you a God-seeker who is conscious of God's existence and hears his spirit telling you to come closer? Do you feel a tugging in your heart to explore God in his fullness? Have you received the witness of salvation and thirst for closer fellowship with God? Then read on; the information following shows what has happened in your wonderful encounter with our divine creator and how to have an intimate relationship with him as you continue on the path of victory.

*Always remember, the word of God is to your spirit
what natural food is to your body. Your spirit
will not survive without God's word.*

CHAPTER 1

A Born-Again Spirit Needs
a New Menu

The experience of receiving Christ Jesus into your heart can be compared to the birth of a baby; in fact, the Bible calls it being born again. As a newborn babe will gradually become aware of his surroundings outside his mother's womb, so the born-again person's spirit becomes alive to the things of God. This new spiritual life must be nurtured by the Word of God and prayer in order for this experience with God to stay alive. First Peter 2:2 says, "As newborn babes, desire the sincere milk of the Word (of God) that ye may grow thereby." You will grow in the knowledge of God as you feed on his word. The daily reading of your Bible will enlighten you about God's plan for your life; Psalm 119:105 says, "Thy word is a lamp unto my feet and a light unto my path." Indeed, the word of God is able to give you a new way of thinking and nourish your spirit all at once. This word of God is the bread your spirit lives on. The renewing of your mind (see Romans 12:2) by reading the word of God empowers your spirit to walk in victory and defeat the devil. Always remember, the word of God is to your spirit as natural food is to your body. Your spirit will not survive without God's word.

Jesus spent much time feeding his spirit with the word of God. In his day, the word of God that was available to him was primarily the Old Testament. His ability to defeat Satan was based on the word of God in him. The quotations that he used to defeat the devil on the mount of temptation—namely, "Man shall not live by bread alone, but by every word that proceedeth out of the mouth of God; thou shall not tempt the Lord thy God; thou shall worship the Lord thy God and Him only shall thou serve"—are all quotations from the book of Deuteronomy in the Old Testament. Like Jesus, we will have to use the word of God to defeat the devil. In fact, we will not be able to defeat him without it.

Prayer is communing with God. It truly connects us to God. Your relationship with the Lord is very personal. You have the right to talk personally to him, and as you pray, your spirit is enlightened so that you can know the Father's will. He has commanded us to ask in prayer. Matthew 7:7 says, "Ask, and it shall be given you; seek, and ye shall find; knock, and it shall be opened unto you." When you are born again, your heart's door is open to God, the Holy Spirit takes up residence in your heart, and prayer becomes life to your spirit as breathing is to your body. Without prayer, the stream of life that flows from God's presence will cease. It is through prayer that you become sensitive to the presence of the Holy Spirit in your heart.

Praying also invites God into the circumstances of our life. This is necessary because when Adam and

Eve sinned in the beginning, they walked away from God's instructions and thereby invited the devil into their world. Since they were the only humans on the planet at that time, the devil got entrance into human affairs. Indeed, it is through this window that Satan got the right to operate in and influence human affairs in this world. The presence of Satan brought sin into the hearts of men, and mankind, like Satan, has been angry and rebellious against God from the first generation that he lived on planet Earth. Yes, it is the same today for so many people.

Enos, the grandson of Adam, was the first man to start an awakening to prayer, which stirred the human race to ask God to return into their affairs. In Genesis 4:25-26, we read, "And Adam knew his wife again: and she bore a son, and called his name Seth: For God, said she, hath appointed me another seed instead of Abel, whom Cain slew. And to Seth, to him also there was born a son and he called his name Enos: then began men to call upon the name of the Lord."

Supporting Scriptures on Growth by the Word of God:

"And he said, so is the kingdom of God, as if a man should cast seed into the ground; and should sleep, and rise night and day, and the seed should spring and grow up, he knoweth not how" (Mark 4:26-27).

"But grow in grace and in the knowledge of our Lord and Savior Jesus Christ. To whom be glory both now and forever" (2 Peter 3:18).

"Jesus answered him saying, it is written, that man shall not live by bread alone but by every word of God" (Luke 4:4).

"But (we) speaking the truth in love, may grow up into Him in all things, which is the head, even Christ" (Ephesians 4:15).

"All scripture is given by inspiration of God and is profitable for doctrine, for reproof, for correction, for instruction in righteousness: that the man of God may be perfect, thoroughly furnished unto all good works" (2 Timothy 3:16-17).

Supporting Scriptures on Prayer:

"O thou that hearest prayer, unto thee shall all flesh come" (Psalm 65:2).

"And all things, whatsoever ye shall ask in prayer, believing, ye shall receive" (Matthew 21:22).

"Is any among you afflicted? Let him pray. Is any merry? Let him sing Psalms. Is any sick among you? Let him call for the elders of the church and let them pray over him, anointing him with oil in the name of the Lord: And the prayer of faith shall save the sick, and the Lord shall raise him up; and if he has committed sins, they shall be forgiven him. Confess your faults one to another, and pray one for another, that ye may be healed. The effectual fervent prayer of a righteous man availeth much" (James 5:13-16).

NOTES

Yes, when Jesus Christ shed his blood on the cross, he deposited into God's heavenly bank all the salvation, benefits, deliverance, and blessings we will ever need.

CHAPTER 2

The New Birth Made Simple

"Therefore, if any man be in Christ, he is a new creation: old things are passed away; behold all things are become new" (2 Corinthians 5:17). In Christ, you are a new creation. You have a recreated spirit, and this is possible because you were transformed (given a spiritual blood transfusion) by the blood of Jesus. It happened the moment you received Jesus as your Savior. When Jesus died on the cross, he took our place of sin, shame, guilt, and condemnation. When we received Christ Jesus, we received his righteousness, and that made us all new in our spirits. Truly, the new birth makes us all citizens of heaven and gives us the right to enjoy all the benefits that Jesus, our heavenly redeemer, bought for us. Philippians 3:20 says, "For our conversation (citizenship) is in heaven; from whence also we look for the Savior, the Lord Jesus Christ."

This experience with Jesus is the most exciting and fulfilling life on this planet. Too many believers have lost these benefits even though they are practicing

Christians. You need to make sure that you do not become a member of this unhappy group.

The blood of Jesus is very important in this process called the new birth. Divine blood was shed when Jesus was punished and crucified. His precious blood was necessary because human blood is contaminated by sin; for all have sinned and come short of the glory of God (Romans 3:23). Mankind's sin-filled blood would not be accepted as a ransom for sin at God's throne. This is the reason why Jesus had to live as the God-man on Planet Earth. The Holy Spirit overshadowed Mary, and she was conceived of the Holy Ghost. This was not the product of man's imagination but a necessary and unavoidable event in the plan of salvation. Jesus took his human nature from the virgin girl and his divine nature from God the Father. In so doing, he got his pure, sinless blood from God the Father. Only God almighty can do that.

After Jesus arose from the grave, his most important mission was to take his sinless blood to the throne of his Father in heaven. That makes clear the reason why Jesus told Mary not to touch him when she saw him just after his resurrection. My friend, if she had touched him, the blood he was taking to his Father's throne would have been contaminated (please read John chapter 20). However, after he returned from the Father later that day, Mary and the disciples were allowed to touch and have fellowship with him. We see a pattern of this in the Old Testament in that no one was allowed to touch the high priest while he was taking the blood of animals into the Holy of Holies, and that place, represented God's presence at that time (please read Leviticus chapter 16).

At the throne of God, Jesus's blood continually cries for mercy on the human race. Whenever you confess faith in the cleansing power of the blood of Jesus or plea the blood of Jesus, you are activating its potential. Make it a habit to plea the blood of Jesus quietly in your heart when situations seem difficult to handle.

As the God-man, Jesus bridged the gap between God and man, and made it possible for us to become sons of God. John 1:12 says, "But as many as received him, to them gave he the power to become the Sons of God, even to them that believe on his name." His divine blood works in four ways: it redeems us, cleanses our spirit, gives us the right of sonship, and removes all the claims of sin and Satan. After you are born again, God does not see your sin; he sees his son's precious blood representing you at his throne.

Many people choose a Christian life that they are comfortable with; they go to church, say a few prayers, give to charity, and do some good works and somehow feel satisfied. It does not matter how great these things appear; they are not the key to a relationship with God. (You may read Luke 18:9-14.) There must be fellowship, which begins with repentance. Repentance involves a change of mind and heart, which has three components: genuine sorrow for wrongs, a sincere decision to change one's life, and the desire in one's heart to be obedient to God. Faith is present at repentance. It originates from our belief in the work of Christ—that is, his shed blood on the cross to free us from our sins. This is the key to a relationship with God, and it does not depend on one being a good person. Many "good people" may end up in hell, as lost souls, if they refuse to accept God's remedy (repentance through faith in the blood of his son) for their sin.

As we continue to walk in the light, the blood of Jesus cleanses us daily. We read in 1 John 1:7, "But if we walk in the light, as He is the light, we have fellowship one with another, and the blood of Jesus Christ, His Son, cleanseth us from all sin." Walking in the light of God's word, which is God himself, establishes our fellowship with him. It is in this fellowship that the blood of Jesus cleanses us daily.

As a new creature in Christ, you can draw on God's blessings and benefits, such as answered prayers, success in your endeavors, financial blessings, healings, and eternal life. These have been made possible for you in Jesus's name. "Do I truly have the right to all of God's blessings and benefits?" you may ask. The answer is yes. God provided all things for you through Christ's death on the cross.

Let me explain this by using an example with which most people are familiar. Suppose someone—for example, Tom—is about to use a check to withdraw $1000.00 from your bank account. Tom will present that check at your bank and the teller will examine the signature and give Tom $1000.00 from your deposit that you made into your account at an earlier date. Your signature gives Tom the right to withdraw money from your account, and the deposit you made earlier provided the funds needed to make the withdrawal possible. In God's economy, the name of Jesus is the signature, name, or authority that authorizes us to withdraw from God's account or benefits, and the blood of Jesus is the deposit that he made on the cross to provide all of the benefits.

Yes, when Jesus Christ shed his blood on the cross, he deposited into God's heavenly bank all the blessings, benefits, deliverance, and salvation we will ever need. Whenever we say, "Father, in Jesus's name I ask that you forgive my sins," or, "Father, in Jesus's name I ask that you heal my body," or make any other request, we are drawing on what Christ Jesus has provided for us in God's heavenly bank. So, be confident in requesting all blessings or benefits from God in the name of Jesus! In John 14:13, Jesus said, "And whatsoever ye shall ask in my name, that will I do, that the father may be glorified in the son."

Some people say, "But I am not righteous enough to receive God's benefits." And truly, by ourselves we will never be able to meet God's righteous requirements, but Jesus is our solution for this problem. He took care of that on the cross by taking our place of sin and shame so that we can have his place of righteousness. He died for our sins. His grace is greater than our shortcomings. Set your heart to do what is right, and the Holy Spirit in you will lead you into green pastures. What if you fail along the way? God always forgives us when we ask him. Micah 7:8 says, "Rejoice not against me, O mine enemy: when I fall, I shall arise; when I sit in darkness, the Lord shall be a light unto me."

Supporting Scriptures on the New Birth:

"Jesus answered and said unto him, verily, verily, I say unto thee, except a man be born again, he cannot see the kingdom of God . . . that which is born of the flesh is flesh; and that which is born of the Spirit is Spirit.

Marvel not that I say unto thee, ye must be born again"
(John 3:3, 6-7).

"And ye hath He quickened, who were dead in trespasses
and sins . . . But God, who is rich in mercy, for His great
love wherewith He loved us, even when we were dead
in sins, hath quickened us together with Christ, (by
grace are ye saved)" (Ephesians 2:1, 4-5).

"That if thou shall confess with thy mouth the Lord
Jesus, and shall believe in thine heart that God hath
raised Him from the dead, thou shall be saved . . . For
whosoever shall call upon the name of the Lord shall be
saved" (Romans 10:9, 13).

"But as many as receive Him, to them give He power
to become the sons of God, even to them that believe
on His name. Which were born, not of blood, nor of the
will of the flesh, nor of the will of man, but of God"
(John 1:12-13).

NOTES

*Water baptism ought to be an exciting activity
in the church and a great event
in the life of every believer.*

CHAPTER 3

Water Baptism; What a Testimony!

Water baptism is one of the ordinances (outward rites) that our Lord Jesus commanded us to perform. It symbolizes the burial of the old life and being raised to the newness of life in Christ and also depicts the death and resurrection of our Savior. Romans 6:4 says, "Therefore we are buried with him by baptism unto death: that like as Christ was raised up from the dead by the glory of the Father, even so we also should walk in the newness of life." This ordinance is a testimony to the world that you are a believer in Christ and that you are not ashamed to be called by his name. Don't ever be ashamed to tell the world that you belong to Jesus. Always remember that he took your shame when he hung on the cross. In Luke 9:26, Jesus said, "If anyone is ashamed of me and my words, the Son of Man will be ashamed of him when He comes in His Glory and of the glory of His Father and of the holy angles"(NIV).

As Peter preached God's word to the first group of Gentile believers, the Holy Spirit fell on them, and he commanded them to be baptized. We read the following in Acts 10:44-48:

> While Peter yet spake these words, the Holy Ghost fell on all them which heard the word. And they of the circumcision which believed were astonished, as many as came with Peter, because that on the Gentiles also was poured out the gift of the Holy Ghost. For they heard them (the Gentiles) speak with tongues, and magnify God. Then answered Peter, can any man forbid water, that these should not be baptized, which have received the Holy Ghost as well as we? And he commanded them to be baptized in the name of the Lord.

Water baptism ought to be an exciting activity in the church and a great event in the life of every believer. Some churches baptize their converts in a pool on the podium after they are saved. Others may take them through a new disciple's class in preparation for baptism. I remember when I was baptized as a young lad, together with a group of believers. Our pastor baptized this group of us young Christians in a small freshwater lake called Lovers Lake. It was surrounded by bushes and trees, with a clear, fresh-water stream flowing in and another flowing out of it. It was the custom for the older saints to stand at the mouth of the lake, singing choruses and praising God while this ordinance was taking place. They sang choruses with lyrics such as "I'm going to lay down my burden, down by the river side." The water was pure and clean, and so was this new experience.

There are often debates about which is the right way to baptize a believer. My suggestion is simple: do it the way Jesus did it. Matthew 3:16 says, "And Jesus, when he was baptized, went up straightway out of the water." To come *up out* of the water, he had to first go down into the water.

Supporting Scriptures on Water Baptism:

Jesus said in Matthew 28:19, "Go ye therefore and teach all nations, baptizing them in the name of the Father, and of the Son, and of the Holy Ghost."

"Then Peter said unto them, repent and be baptized every one of you in the name of Jesus Christ for the remission of sins, and ye shall receive the gift of the Holy Ghost; For this promise is unto you, and to your children, and to all that are a far off, even as many as the Lord our God shall call. And with many other words did he testify and exhort, saying, save yourself from this untoward generation. Then they that gladly received the word were baptized: and the same day there were added unto them about three thousand souls" (Acts 2:38-41).

"And as they went on their way, they came unto certain water: and the eunuch said, see, here is water: what does hinder me to be baptized? And Philip said, If thou believest with all thine heart, thou mayest. And he answered and said, I believe that Jesus Christ is the son of God. And he commanded the chariot to stand still: and they went down both into the water, both Philip and the eunuch; and he baptized him" (Acts 8:36-38).

NOTES

NOTES

God never intended for you to be a Lone Ranger Christian. Your survival and success as a Christian depends greatly on your fellowship with those who are a part of the Lord, and the redeemed members of the local church are a part of him.

CHAPTER 4

The Local Church Is an Exciting Place to Grow

When we confess our sins to Christ, we are born again and we need to get connected to our new family called the local church. Some people call it joining the church or getting religion. The local church is where believers come together in their immediate community to receive fellowship and much-needed help so that they can mature into the image of Christ. We need to have some basic instructions if we are to be successful Christians. Some of these instructions we will never receive unless another believer in Jesus Christ teaches us. God has set it up this way. This has been so from the very beginning of man's relationship with God.

Moses was one of the greatest prophets ever. He spoke to God mouth-to-mouth (Numbers 12:5-8), but he needed the advice of his father-in-law to be successful in leading the children of Israel to the Promised Land. In Exodus 18:14-24, it says:

And when Moses' father in law saw all that he
did to the people, he said, what is this thing
that thou doest to this people? Why sittest thou
thyself alone, and all the people stand by thee
from morning to even? And Moses said unto his
father-in-law, because the people come unto
me to enquire of God: When they have a matter,
they come unto me; and I judge between one and
another, and I do make them know the statutes
of God, and his laws. And Moses father in law said
unto him, the thing that thou doest is not good.
Thou shall surely wear away, both thou, and this
people that is with thee: for the thing is too heavy
for thee; thou art not able to perform it thyself
alone. Hearken now unto my voice, and I will
give thee counsel, and God shall be with thee: Be
thou for the people to Godard, that thou mayest
bring the causes unto God: And thou shall teach
them ordinances and laws, and shall show them
the way wherein they must walk, and the work
that they must do. Moreover thou shall provide
out of all the people able men, such as fear God,
men of truth, hating covetousness; and place such
over them, to be rulers of thousands, and rulers of
hundreds, rulers of fifties and rulers of tens. And
let them Judge the people at all seasons; and it
shall be, that every great matter they shall bring
unto thee, but every small matter they shall judge:
so shall it be easier for thyself, and they shall bear
the burden with thee. If thou do this thing and
God command thee so, then thou shall be able to
endure, and all this people shall also go to their

place in peace. So Moses harkened to the voice of
his Father-in-law, and did all that he had said.

The local Christian church began in Acts chapter
2. In verse forty-seven of this chapter, we read, "And
the Lord added to the church daily such as should be
saved." In Hebrews 10:25, the Bible further says, "Not
forsaking the assembling of ourselves together, as the
manner of some is; but exhorting one another: and
so much the more, as you see the day approaching."
The assembling of ourselves for worship is a command
of God, and those who refuse to do so are living in
disobedience. God never intended for you to be a
Lone Ranger Christian. Your survival and success as a
Christian depends greatly on your fellowship with those
who are a part of the Lord, and the redeemed members
of the local church are a part of him. Many talk shows
on television are saying you do not need to go to church
and you can have church by yourself in your home, but
this is not what the Bible teaches. You will not be able
to survive and become a strong Christian all alone or
even with your immediate family.

Yes, you need a pastor who works with trusted and
respectful leaders in your local assembly where you
choose to have fellowship, and with whom you can
discuss problems and other matters. God has given
gifted leaders to the local church for this purpose.
There will be times in your Christian walk when the
advice of the pastor or an elder will be invaluable.
Proverbs 22:20 says, "Have not I written to thee
excellent things in counsels and knowledge." Counsel
and knowledge are necessary for our natural life as well
as our spiritual walk. There will be occasions when you

will need instructions that are exclusively for you and very specific in nature. Direct connection with a leader will help to meet this need.

Jesus always sent his disciples out two by two. He set this pattern not only for the ministry of the word but also for natural things, such as to fetch him an ass on Palm Sunday or to buy some Passover bread; please read Matthew 21:1-3. No one was meant to handle life's challenges alone. Ecclesiastes 4:9 says, "Two are better than one, because they have a good reward for their labor." When Adam was alone in the garden, the Lord God said, "It is not good that the man should be alone; I will make a help meet (not help *meat* but help *meet*) for him." Jesus needed Simon of Cyrene to help him with his cross. If he had refused that help, he and the cross would not have made it to Golgotha's hill.

And we need be open-hearted and teachable as we fellowship with others. It is good to approach every situation as a potential learning experience. God has given to every believer an individual gift or talent, and there is quite a lot that we need to learn from each other.

Beware of wrong habits and bad company in the local church. Some people are very good at pointing out all the perceived faults of the pastor without realizing that he will not be most excellent at everything. And the pastor's vantage point of looking at a matter may quite often be much different. This is so because the church's functions are generally structured for the salvation, help, and love of people rather than to do things the world's way, which is governed by profit and loss. In my Christian walk, I have served and worked with many pastors, and each one has shown some shortcomings, but God has blessed and taught me through them all.

You will learn to do by doing simple things. Be willing to help even when you are not asked to assist. To develop in your local assembly, you will need to get involved in the activities of your church. Your prayers and financial support for your church and pastor are two of the most important contributions you can offer. Nothing should be too insignificant for you to do if it will help another person in his fellowship with God. Many great preachers can recall their divine experiences while mopping floors and cleaning the toilets of their local assembly. Quite often, it was while doing these menial tasks that God visited them. The Prophet Samuel was a servant boy in the household of Eli the Priest when God called him. Jesus said, "He that is faithful in that which is least, is faithful also in much: and he that is unjust in that which is least is unjust also in much" (Luke 16:10). He further declared, "He that is greatest among you shall be your servant" (Matthew 23:11).

The immediate community of the local church can encompass a much wider radius today when compared to the early Christian assembly recorded in the Bible. This is possible in part because of the present-day efficiency and speed with which people can move from one neighborhood to another. The existence of cathedrals and mega-churches that represent local congregations in our cities might not have been possible without these two factors. Do not be overburdened if the size of your local fellowship is small. There were both small and large churches in the New Testament. The first church was started in Jerusalem, with about three thousand believers (Acts 2:41), and, by comparison, the Apostle Paul sent greetings to a disciple by the name of Nymphas, in the city of Laodicea, who had a church in his house. This shows that you can experience God in a cathedral as well as in a house meeting. We are called to serve God, not a building!

Five Important Benefits of Assembling Together:

1) You are taught the word of God by the leaders of the assembly so that you can grow in the image of Christ.
2) Christian brothers and sisters will assist you in prayer, especially in times of trial. Be aware, you will need this help.
3) Being a part of this corporate body makes you a contributor to its effort to win lost souls for Jesus.
4) You have a pastor, who watches for you as a shepherd watches over his flock.
5) This surrounding will help to prepare you for your divine assignment through the experience and blessings you receive.

Do not forget that the devil is out to get you. This is not meant to make you fearful, but it's a caution so that you will not be careless. First Peter 5:8-9 says, "Be sober, be vigilant, because your adversary, the devil, like a roaring lion walketh about seeking whom he may devour: whom resist steadfastly in the faith." Always remember that Satan is like a roaring lion, but his teeth were pulled and his power was destroyed by our Lord Jesus when he came up out of the grave as the resurrected Savior. Colossians 2:15 says, Jesus spoiled principalities and powers and made a show of them openly, triumphing over them in the process. Principalities and powers represent the highest-ranking spirits in Satan's kingdom, and we rule over them In Jesus' name.

In Ephesians 4:11-14 we read the following:

And He (Christ) gave some, apostles; and some, prophets; and some, evangelists; and some, pastors, and teachers; for the perfecting of the saints, for the work of the ministry, for the edifying of the body of Christ. Till we all come in the unity of the faith, and of the knowledge of the Son of God, unto a perfect man, unto the measure of the stature of the fullness of Christ. That we henceforth be no more children, tossed to and fro, and carried about with every wind of doctrine, by the sleight of men, and cunning craftiness, by which they lie in wait to deceive.

If you read the fourth chapter of the book of Ephesians, you will notice that it was after Jesus was raised up from the dead that he gave these ministries. The persons God places in these offices are there to teach and guide the church. Correct teaching and instruction in the ways of the Lord will help young Christians to grow up quickly. Doctrinal error and wrong advice can cause unnecessary pain and hardship, and many nonproductive and wasteful years, even though an individual may be born again and baptized in the Holy Spirit. Do you know that doctrinal difference is a main contributor to there being so many different Christian denominations today?

Your local church is the place where you become qualified for God's promotion. It is in this atmosphere that you can mature in Christ. There is a time for you to receive milk—that is, the simple teachings from God's word—before you are able to use the solid food, or stronger doctrinal truths. The stronger teachings will enable you to endure hardship like a trained soldier in God's army. You are not qualified to lead until you have learned the art of following a leader. You will not achieve much if you are not trained by a successful warrior. God uses men to mentor other humans. Your pastor or leader should be your closest example of a victorious soldier.

I need to emphasize that the two important distinctions that will help you to qualify for higher offices in God's local church are your services—first, to your local assembly; and second, to God's anointed servant (in most cases, he will be your pastor). Joshua was a dedicated servant to Moses before God chose him to lead the children of Israel. Elisha was a dedicated servant to Elijah before God chose him to be prophet in Elijah's stead. Paul was serving faithfully in the church at Antioch when God called him to fulfill his apostolic ministry.

We read the following in Acts 13:1-4:

Now there were in the church that was at Antioch certain prophets and teachers, as Barnabas, and Simeon, who is called Niger, and Lucius of Cyrene, and Manaen who had been brought up with Herod, the tetrarch, and Saul. As they ministered to the Lord, and fasted, the Holy Spirit said, separate me Barnabas and Saul for the work unto which I have called them. And when they had fasted and prayed and laid their hands on them, they sent them away. So they, being sent forth by the Holy Spirit, departed unto selucia; and from there they sailed to Cyprus.

Please note that it was the elders of the church at Antioch who laid their hands on Barnabas and Saul (also known as Paul) and released them into their divine calling. The statement in this passage, "So they, being sent forth by the Holy Spirit," was possible because they qualified themselves in their local church. God's blessing is on everyone who has been commissioned to a new assignment by the elders of his local church after that person has served faithfully.

Supporting Scriptures on the Local Church:

Paul told the leaders of the Church in Ephesus, "Take heed therefore to yourselves, and to all the flock over which the Holy Ghost hath made you overseers, to feed the church of God, which He hath purchased with His own blood" (Acts 20:28).

Many churches started in homes. We see in 1 Corinthians 16:19, "The churches of Asia salute you. Aquila and Priscilla salute you much in the Lord, with the church that is in their house."

"Salute the brethren which are in Laodicea, and Nymphas, and the church which is in his house" (Colossians 4:15).

"How is it then brethren? When ye come together, every one of you hath a Psalm, hath a doctrine, hath a tongue, hath a revelation, and hath an interpretation. Let everything be done unto edifying" (1 Corinthians 14:26).

"And they continued daily in one accord in the temple, and breaking bread from house to house, did eat their meat with gladness and singleness of heart, praising God and having favor with all the people. And the Lord added to the church daily such as should be saved" (Acts 2:46-47).

"Not forsaking the assembling of ourselves together, as the manner of some is, but exhorting one another, and so much the more, as you see the day approaching" (Hebrews 10:25).

NOTES

At the new birth, the Holy Spirit comes into the heart; whereas, at the baptism in the Holy Spirit, he comes upon the believer. These different experiences can be compared to having your cup filled with water as a onetime experience and having the same cup overflow under a running tap.

CHAPTER 5

Baptism in the Holy Spirit Is Glorious and Powerful

You were born of the Spirit when you confessed your sins to God, and Christ, in the person of the Holy Spirit, came into your heart. The baptism of the Holy Spirit is a baptism of power when the Holy Spirit comes upon you. This can take place at the moment of the new birth or at a later time, but it must be clear that it is different from the experience of the new birth.

In Acts 1:8, Jesus said to his disciples, "But ye shall receive power, after that the Holy Ghost is come upon you: and ye shall be witnesses unto me both in Jerusalem, and in all Judaea, and in Samaria and unto the uttermost part of the earth." When Jesus said this, the disciples already had the Holy Spirit, but they were not baptized in it. We know this from the record in John 20:19-23:

> Then the same day at evening, being the first day of the week, when the doors were shut where

the disciples were assembled for fear of the Jews, came Jesus and stood in the midst, and saith unto them, "Peace be unto you." And when He had so said he shewed unto them his hands and his side. Then were the disciples glad, when they saw the Lord. Then said Jesus to them again, "Peace be unto you: as my father hath sent me, even so sent I you." And when he had said this, he breathed on them, and saith unto them, "Receive ye the Holy Ghost: Whosesoever sins ye remit, they are remitted unto them; and whosesoever sins ye retain, they are retained."

Breathing on the disciples was the first operation of Jesus after he was resurrected from the dead; he breathed the Holy Spirit on the disciples. This operation is recorded in the preceding passage. It had never taken place in human history. Before this operation, God's spirit upon men for a particular task; as in the case of Sampson in Judges 14: 6, 19 and 15:14, but it was not breathed on (into) them.

Let us read it again for emphasis and clarity; verse 22 says, "And when he had said this, he breathed on them, and saith unto them, 'Receive ye the Holy Ghost.'" What the disciples received at that time was the indwelling of the Holy Spirit as their sins were remitted, pardoned, or forgiven. In other words, they received the new birth. Thirty-nine days later, however, Jesus commanded the disciples to wait for the promise (baptism in the Holy Spirit) of the Father. We can see clearly that this promise is an additional experience in the Holy Spirit. I do have to say further: at the new birth, the Holy Spirit comes *into* the heart, whereas at the baptism in the Holy Spirit, he comes upon the believer. These different experiences can be compared to having your cup filled with water as a onetime experience and having the same cup overflow under a running tap. In John 7:38, Jesus said, "He that believeth on me, as the scripture hath said, out of his belly shall flow rivers of living water."

Baptism in the Holy Spirit is not possible if one is not born (born again) of the Spirit, and this baptism can be received by the laying on of hands, although this is not always necessary. In Acts 8:14-17, we read,

> *Now when the Apostles who were at Jerusalem heard that Samaria had received the word of God, they sent unto them Peter and John: who, when they were come down, prayed for them, that they might receive the Holy Ghost; (for as yet He had fallen upon none of them: only they were baptized in the name of the Lord Jesus). Then laid they their hands on them and they received the Holy Ghost.*

Two keys that will open the door for anyone to receive the baptism in the Holy Spirit are correct knowledge about the Holy Spirit and hunger for the word of God (the truth of God). God does not bless ignorance: you need to know that you can be baptized in the Holy Spirit, and your hunger for righteousness creates the vacuum that he fills. Matthew 5:6 says, "Blessed are they who hunger and thirst after righteousness, for they shall be filled." Christians who say, "I do not believe the baptism in the Holy Spirit is for today," or, "I do not want to be baptized in the Holy Spirit," are not suitable candidates for this experience.

I am of the conviction that most Christians who receive the Holy Spirit's baptism of power do not tap into the full potential they can receive from him. This is similar to what happens in everyday life; someone receives a gift and places it on a shelf of his home, leaving it to acquire dust and rust, and another person receives the same gift, explores its potential, and uses it to do great things. A great potential is created the moment the Holy Spirit comes upon the believer, but it must be explored.

The initial evidence of the baptism in the Holy Spirit is speaking in tongues. This occurred when the Holy Spirit was poured for the first time onto the believing Jews. In Acts 2:2-4, the Bible says, "And suddenly there came a sound from heaven as of a rushing mighty wind and it filled all the house where they were sitting. And there appeared unto them cloven tongues like as of fire and it sat upon each of them. And they were all filled with the Holy Ghost and began to speak with other tongues as the Spirit gave them utterance." Speaking in tongues was also the initial evidence when the first Gentile believers received the Holy Ghost. In Acts 10: 45-47, the Bible says, "And they of the circumcision which believe were astonished, as many as came with Peter because that on the Gentiles also was poured out the gift of the Holy Ghost. For they heard them speak with tongues, and magnified God. Then answered Peter, can any man forbid water, that these should not be baptized, which have received the Holy Ghost as well as we?"

This initial evidence of the baptism in the Holy Ghost has other witnesses. In Acts 19:6, the Bible says, "And when Paul had laid his hands upon them. The Holy

Ghost came on them; and they spake with tongues and prophesied." The sorcerer Simon saw initial evidence when the Apostles Peter and John laid their hands on the believers so that they might receive the baptism in the Holy Ghost. Simon wanted this ability and offered them money on condition that they give him this gift (Acts 8:9-24).

After we are baptized in the Holy Spirit, his gifts and power, which are also evidence of this experience, will take some time to develop in us. The extent of their development depends on how obedient and yielded we are to him. The Holy Spirit is a person, not a thing; he completes the Trinity, which includes the Father and the Son. If we ask him for help in developing his gifts in us, he will help us. The person who follows the Lord with all his heart and yields graciously for the development of his new life in the Spirit will eventually show the manifestation of the gifts and power of the Holy Spirit. For about four decades I have noticed three important characteristics of people who get saved and receive the baptism of the Holy Spirit.

- First, the manifestation of speaking in other tongues is the initial evidence of their experience.
- Second, they do not backslide easily.
- Third, they are more likely to believe God for greater supernatural manifestations, such as healing and miracles, than other Christians who do not have this experience.

Quite recently, the Lord spoke something into my spirit that brought great confidence into my heart, and it is this: "For millennia, the devil has established great religions and concepts in the world in an effort to control the minds and lifestyles of all people. It is not possible to defeat these concepts and ideas with human wisdom, but, with the power and gifts of the Holy Spirit, it can be done." The baptism in the Holy Spirit makes us empowered witnesses of the resurrected Lord, and through this power, we are defeating all the works of darkness.

Jesus told the disciples to wait for the promise of the Father or the baptism in the Holy Ghost. In Acts chapter 2, the promise came, and the disciples were never the same. Peter stood up and spoke the word of God with the Holy Ghost's boldness, and three thousand souls were the first converts of the first church. In Acts chapters 3 and 4, miracles and healings flowed, and five thousand men were added to the disciples. Great manifestations of the power of the Holy Ghost took place, and the church demonstrated an anointing to deal with every situation. Praise God!

This power is still available today: "For the promise is unto you, and unto your children, and to all that are afar off, even as many as the Lord our God shall call" (Acts 2:39). What hinders most Christians from doing these mighty works? I would suggest four things: namely religion, the ideas of men, laziness, and silence. Religious doctrines have kept Christians in a box for too long. The ideas of men, instead of what the Bible says, have been obstacles in the way of the operations and moves of the Holy Ghost. Laziness or the unwillingness to seek God's presence is also an existing factor. Silence or lack of preaching about the supernatural power of God has grieved the spirit. We have to preach, teach, and exercise ourselves in the supernatural for it to operate. If we stop proclaiming the supernatural, it will cease to operate among us, and God will find some simple, just-converted sinners to believe him and demonstrate it. It is time for a change; let's join the group that is seeking the face of God with no reservations!

Supporting Scriptures on the Baptism in the Holy Spirit:

"And be not drunk with wine, wherein is excess; but be filled with the Spirit. Speaking to yourselves in psalms and hymns and spiritual songs, singing and making melody in your heart to the Lord. Giving thanks always for all things unto God and the Father in the name of our Lord Jesus Christ" (Ephesians 5:18-20).

"And it shall come to pass afterward, that I will pour out my Spirit upon all flesh: your sons and your daughters shall prophesy, your old men shall dream dreams, your young men shall see visions. And also upon the servants and upon the handmaids in those days will I pour out my Spirit" (Joel 2:28-29).

"And suddenly there came a sound from heaven as of a rushing mighty wind, and it filled the entire house where they were sitting. And there appeared unto them cloven tongues like as of fire, and it sat upon each of them. And they were all filled with the Holy Ghost, and began to speak with other tongues as the Spirit gave them utterance" (Acts 2:2-4).

"And when Paul had laid his hands on them, the Holy Ghost came on them: and they spake with tongues and prophesied" (Acts 19:6).

NOTES

Financial success always follows a season of faithful giving. In some believers' experience, it has taken months; in others', a much shorter time. This success will always come to the expectant heart. That is truly my testimony.

CHAPTER 6

Do Not Eat the Seed You Need to Plant

In Genesis 8:22, God made a promise to Noah that belongs to all generations. He said, "While the earth remaineth, seedtime and harvest, and cold and heat, and summer and winter, and day and night shall not cease." The principle of *seedtime and harvest* mentioned in this verse extends into giving and forms the foundation of it. Whenever you give of your substance to your church or any ministry, remember that you are giving to the Lord. You could have spent the money on something personal, but rather, you chose to plant it as seed in the work of the Lord. Our God will bless you accordingly. Yes, God promises to reward you, but let love be the motivation behind all your sacrificial gifts to him. He promises that whatever you sow in love to him and his work, he will return to you, multiplied many times over.

There are some people who say that they do not want or expect God to give them anything in return for their tithes and offerings, but that may be foolish pride. It is God who offers to increase and multiply what we give (Malachi 3: 10-12). We can recognize this principle throughout the Bible, and we ought not to insult his offer and wisdom. People do not work for their employers and expect nothing in return. Is the almighty God less generous than human employers? No! He giveth us richly all things to enjoy (1 Timothy 6: 17B). Our earthly fathers are very pleased to give us gifts and wonderful things, especially when we honor them. God, our heavenly Father, is no different. He expressly stated that we need to honor him with our gifts and promises us thirty, sixty, and one hundred fold return. Praise God; he is more than generous!

Look carefully at your church's teaching about giving and examine the matter in your Bible to see the truth about it. You need to expect a harvest as you give your tithes, which belong to your local assembly, and your offerings. Offerings may be given as the Lord leads. Your harvest may take time and appear in many forms (financial, health, family blessings, business success, victory over the devil, and more); just remain faithful. Financial success always follows a season of faithful giving. In some believers' experience it has taken months; in others', a much shorter time. This success will always come to the expectant heart. That is truly my testimony.

In Malachi 3:10-12, we read,

> *Bring ye all the tithes into the storehouse, that there may be meat in my house, and prove me now herewith, saith the Lord of hosts, if I will not open you the windows of heaven and pour you out a blessing, that there shall not be room enough to receive it. I will rebuke the*

*devourer for your sakes, and he shall not destroy the
fruits of your ground; neither shall your vine cast her
fruit before the time in the field, saith the Lord of hosts.
And all nations shall call you blessed: for ye shall be a
delightsome land, saith the Lord of hosts.*

The seven blessings one receives from giving tithes and
offerings are as follows:

1) "Open you the windows of heaven" (verse 10): speaks of revival, renewal, and spiritual refreshing.
2) "Pour you out a blessing, that there shall not be room enough to receive" (verse 10): says that there will eventually be abundance and prosperity in your life.
3) "Rebuke the devourer for your sakes" (verse 11): explains how Satan is crippled in every area of your life.
4) "He shall not destroy the fruits of your ground" (verse 11): declares success in your business and industry.
5) "Neither shall your vine cast her fruit before the time in the field" (verse 12): guarantees the prosperity and security for your children.
6) "Nations shall call you blessed" (verse 12): says you will receive honors and goodwill from strangers and foreigners.
7) "Ye shall be a delightsome land" (verse 12): says exciting discoveries, divine favor, joy, creativity, and a pleasant atmosphere will be with you.

Do you notice that the expression *"saith the Lord of hosts"* is mentioned three times in the original passage with these promises and blessings? Yes, it is written once in each verse. This means that the Lord guarantees they will come to pass. In verse 10, God challenges us to prove him faithful in doing his part as we obey his command to give. I do not readily recall any other passage in the Bible where God said to prove him. As you tithe and give your offering, please do not forget to thank God in anticipation of the manifestation of his blessings and promises. In time, they will show up in every area of your life. Some people's waiting period for these blessings are longer than others, and there may be many reasons why this is so. Please remember that our God, who cannot lie, always keeps his side of the agreement.

Supporting Scriptures on Giving:

"Cast thy bread upon the waters: for thou shall find it after many days. Give a portion to seven, and also to eight; for thou knowest not what evil shall be upon the earth" (Ecclesiastes 11:1-2).

"Give, and it shall be given unto you; good measure, pressed down, shaken together, and running over, shall men give into your bosom. For with the same measure that you mete withal it shall be measured to you again" (Luke 6:38).

"But this I say, that he which soweth sparingly shall reap also sparingly; and he which soweth bountifully shall reap also bountifully" (2 Corinthians 9:6).

"And this stone, which I have set for a pillar, shall be God's house: and of all that thou shall give me I will surely give the Tenth unto thee" (Genesis 28:22).

"And concerning the tithe of the herd, or of the flock, even of whatsoever passeth under the rod, the tenth shall be holy unto the Lord" (Leviticus 27:32).

NOTES

NOTES

It is recorded that the sixteenth president of these United States, President Abraham Lincoln (1809-1865), spent much time meditating on the holy scriptures, especially during the Civil War years.

CHAPTER 7

Winning the Battle in the Mind

The mind is the battlefield of every believer; it is the gate through which thoughts flow in favor of or against God's righteous counsel. If evil thoughts are allowed to develop in our minds, they will produce sin and can lead to death in our spirit. Righteous thoughts that are based on the word of God will produce faith in our spirit and will lead us to life and victory in Christ.

The believer's mind is not redeemed; it is renewed daily by the word of God. Romans 12:2 says, "And be not conformed to this world but be ye transformed by the renewing of your mind, that ye may prove what is that good, and acceptable, and perfect, will of God." Before we were born again, our minds were programmed to think in line with the counsel and systems of the world. The mind-set we developed from our past life without Christ must be changed if we are to please God. How can we do this? By *reading*, *meditating*, and *memorizing* the word of God. And this can be and ought to be done with great joy. Psalm 119:111 says, "Thy testimonies have I taken as a heritage for ever: for they are the rejoicing of my heart."

Reading the word of God is vital for our survival and should be done on a daily basis. You may use a Bible-reading guide, develop a personal reading plan, or follow suggestions from your bishop or pastor. Whatever you do, make sure you read God's word. There are immeasurable benefits in doing so. These benefits include growing up in the image of Christ, feeding your spirit so that you can be strong to resist temptations, knowing God's promises so that you can claim them, and praying with the knowledge of his word.

Meditating on God's word takes you a lot higher. This is a private devotional act, consisting of deliberate reflection upon some spiritual truth or mystery. It is best to do so with a great desire to act on the revelations God gives you. You are not in a hurry to rush through the scriptures you are examining, and you are spending much more time giving them extended thought. This can take hours and even days. During this exercise, an ordinary verse of the Bible can reveal deeper and more profound truth. It will help you to receive many specific revelations and insights God wants to make clear to you.

It is recorded that the sixteenth president of these United States, President Abraham Lincoln (1809-1865), spent much time meditating on the holy scriptures, especially during the Civil War years. These scriptures were no doubt a source of strength and assurance to the president at a time when the country was being ripped apart by a war that caused the death of about six hundred and twenty thousand Americans from ammunitions and disease. Historians recorded that

President Lincoln's knowledge of the Bible was so thorough that his political opponents generally found themselves on dangerous grounds when they quoted it against him.

Strive to be the Christian who will not settle for mediocre experiences. Learn to spend time meditating on God's word, and you will receive such great understanding that others may label you super spiritual even though you know that you are not. Many years ago, I conducted an exercise of meditating, studying, and cross-referencing scriptures about the heart (the Bible's concept of), and it was amazing what great truths I discovered. If you do the same on any topic, you will be amazed.

Reading the word loudly to yourself is another form of meditation and can be amazingly powerful, especially at times when your mind is under attack or you are experiencing some difficulty. Indeed, it is a sure way of regaining control of your mind when you are hard-pressed by circumstances. The words of scripture that you read loudly are more powerful than any confusing thought coming against your mind. Hebrews 4:12 says it this way: "For the word of God is living, and powerful, and sharper than any two-edged sword, piercing even to the dividing asunder of the soul and spirit, and of the joints and marrow, and is a discerner of the thoughts and intent of the heart."

Please do not try meditating on the word of God when you know that you are living in rebellion to our Lord Jesus. Meditation that invokes revelations from the throne of God will only illuminate a heart that is washed in the blood of Jesus. This is not an effort to bring you into self-condemnation, but remember that the mysteries and insights of God flow freely into a pure heart. People practicing meditation without the right heart can open themselves to demon spirits

Memorizing the word is also very important. In this process, you can endeavor to store verses of the Bible in your memory for future use. It increases your ability to use the word of God as the sword of the spirit. This makes you a vicious and victorious warrior against the devil. Jesus's memory of God's word brought him great victory while in combat with the devil at the mount of temptation. At times, you will be in situations where you do not have ready access to a Bible, and your memory of the word will not only help you overcome a test but also strengthen you to wage a decisive victory against the enemy.

If you desire to be a strong Christian, you need to develop a stock of scripture or Bible verses that you will store in your memory as a reservoir. Developing this treasure is not a burdensome task because the Holy Spirit will help you to remember these verses when you need them most.

Eight scriptures that I have learned to love and can recite from memory are:

i) "Ye are of God, little children, and have overcome them: because greater is he that is in you, than he that is in the world" (1 John 4:4).

Here we see that Christ the mightier one lives in us.

ii) "Who (God) forgives all thine iniquities; who healeth all thy diseases" (Psalm 103:3).

This verse gives confidence to those who worry about receiving healing even though they know that God has forgiven their sins.

iii) "For God so loved the world that He gave His only begotten son that whosoever believeth in Him shall not perish but have everlasting life" (John 3:16).

Quote this scripture when you are sharing your faith on a person-to-person basis. Many people will tell you that they know this verse, John 3:16; the question to ask is, "Do you know the God of John 3:16?"

iv) "Therefore if any man be in Christ, he is a new creature: old things are passed away; behold all things are become new" (2 Corinthians 5:17).

From this passage, we understand that we are not bound by any wrongdoing in the past and that we have all of God's benefits and goodness available to us.

v) "The thief cometh not, but for to steal, and to kill, and to destroy: I am come that they might have life, and that they might have it more abundantly" (John 10:10).

I remember memorizing this verse as a young Christian, and its enlightenment has not left me for over thirty-five years. I saw that Satan was the source of all stealing, killing, and evil, and our God was the source of all goodness and life.

vi) "But they that wait upon the Lord shall renew their strength; they shall mount up with wings like eagles;

they shall run and not be weary; and they shall walk and not faint" (Isaiah 40:31).

Here we see that seeking the Lord brings a new lease on life and unlimited possibilities.

vii) "Casting all your care upon him; for he careth for you" (1 Peter 5:7).

This promise encourages us to live a burden-free life in a problem-filled world by putting all of our cares upon Jesus.

viii) "I can do all things through Christ which strengthens me" (Philippians 4:13).

The passage really means that you can do all things through Christ's anointing in you. It is not referring to Christ the person doing all things through you, but rather you doing all things through the level of the power (anointing) of Christ in you.

At the end of this book, I have added some choice passages of scripture from the Psalms and the Epistles, with the objective of developing in you a desire for reading, meditating on, and memorizing the word of God.

NOTES

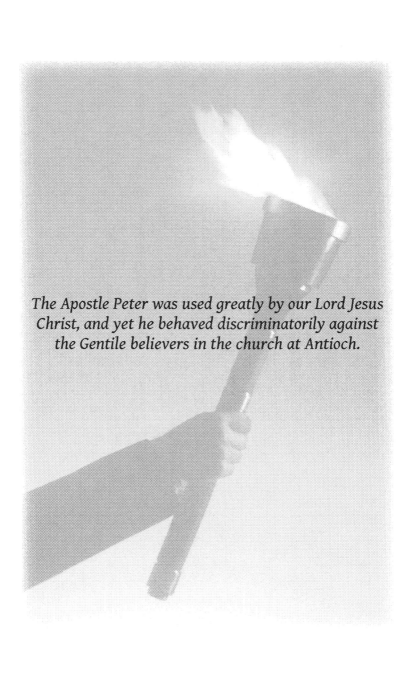

The Apostle Peter was used greatly by our Lord Jesus Christ, and yet he behaved discriminatorily against the Gentile believers in the church at Antioch.

CHAPTER 8

Bumps in Our Path Can Strengthen and Develop Us

Yes, you will encounter trials, tests, and temptations as you live for the Lord. They can come through many sources, including family, friends, strangers, church members, workmates, enemies, and, of course, the devil. When you are tempted, always remember that the Greater One lives in you. First John 4:4 says, "Ye are of God, little children, and have overcome them (the world, the flesh, and the devil); because greater is he that is in you, than he that is in the world." And Psalm 34:17-19 says, "The righteous cry, and the Lord heareth, and delivereth them out of all their troubles. The Lord is nigh unto them that are of a broken heart; and saveth such as be of a contrite spirit. Many are the afflictions of the righteous: but the Lord delivereth him out of them all."

Indeed, you will be tested and tried, sometimes in your local church. Many people have turned away from following our Lord because they encounter unpleasant situations with other believers in their local assembly.

We may reason that this ought not to be, but sometimes it happens.

The Apostle Peter was used greatly by our Lord Jesus Christ, and yet he behaved very discriminatorily against the Gentiles believers in the church at Antioch. Paul, the seemingly younger apostle, had to correct the Apostle Peter openly. In Galatians 2:11-14, we read the following:

> But when Peter was come to An-ti-och, I withstood him to the face, because he was to be blamed. For before that certain men came from James, he did eat with the Gentiles: but when they were come, he withdrew and separated himself, fearing them which were of the circumcision. And the other Jews dissembled likewise with him; insomuch that Barnabas also was carried away with their dissimulation. But when I saw that they walked not uprightly according to the truth of the gospel, I said unto Peter before them all, "If thou being Jew livest after the manner of Gentiles, and not as do the Jews, why compellest thou the Gentiles to live as do the Jews?"

Friend, God may use someone to do a great job for him, but that does not change that person from being a human being with shortcomings. Do not let anyone (including a pastor or leader) or anything stop you from following the Lord. We are not followers of mere men but of Jesus, the Son of God. Let us keep our eyes on our Heavenly Leader so that when our earthly leaders fail, we will not walk away from the faith. Please note that the Apostle Peter was very repentant of his wrongdoing.

He later referred to the Apostle Paul as a man of great wisdom and revelation (2 Peter 3:15-16).

Each test or temptation you face should be seen as a stepping stone for promotion to greater things. Can you remember when you were in school or college and you had to face those exams and papers? Preparing for and doing them were not usually enjoyable, but after they were over and you got good grades, you were happy and ready for celebration and promotion. I recently reminded my daughter that a test is given to see what you have learned and if you are ready for advancement.

God will not always shield us from testing and temptation; he will make a way of escape, but the final decision is ours. Look at Adam's temptation in the garden (Genesis chapter 3); he failed and lost his position in the universe. Can you imagine what would have happened if Adam had said no to the devil's enticement in the Garden of Eden? There would have been no sickness, disease, poverty, and death. Adam would have been alive today, exploring the vastness of God's universe. We would not have had to fear congestion. Some people might have been living on the moon, exploring the universe from there. There is room in this world for everyone, and the universe is expanding at the speed of light. Use your imagination!

If we look at Jesus's temptation in the wilderness, which is recorded in Luke chapter 4, we will notice that he overcame his tests. Jesus is presently reigning over Satan, his demons, and the entire universe. Philippians 2:9-11 says, "Wherefore God also hath highly exalted him (Christ), and hath given him a name which is above every name: that at the name of Jesus every knee should bow, of things in heaven, and things on earth, and things under the earth; and that every tongue should confess that Jesus Christ is Lord to the glory of God the Father."

During temptation, you need to use the word of God as your weapon to defeat the devil. When you are tempted to be afraid, quote 2 Timothy 1:7: "For God hath not given us the spirit of fear; but of power, and of love, and of a sound mind."

You may be tempted to doubt your salvation and freedom from sin; quote Psalm 103:12: "As far as the east is from the west, so far hath He removed our transgression from us."

When sickness and disease come against you, use scriptures such as Psalm 103:2-3: "Bless the Lord, O my soul, and forget not all his benefits: Who forgiveth all thine iniquities; who healeth all thy diseases."

NOTES

The emphasis placed on Jim Jones and his goodness,
with no reference to the person of Christ and
his work, was very disturbing to me.

CHAPTER 9

Experience the Joy of Sharing Your Faith

J esus commissioned every Christian to strive to win the lost. In Mark 16:15, we read, "And he said unto them, 'Go ye into all the world, and preach the gospel to every creature.'" The greatest act you can perform as a Christian is to obey Jesus's command to share him with others. The easiest way to share Jesus is by the testimony of your conversion. Many Christians hesitate to share Christ because they think that they do not have a great testimony or know enough about the Christian life. May I say that you do have a great testimony! To be born again is the greatest testimony anyone can have. Testifying of your conversion is relating your supernatural experience with God, and that opens the door to all other testimonies.

It is wise for a young Christian to start sharing his faith in small and simple ways; begin with your friends and family, but do not expect smooth sailing. You may be laughed at or even cursed out. Do not be discouraged. As you keep telling others about God's goodness, he will put words and messages into your heart. You may not know what to say, but the Holy Spirit does. Some of the greatest revelations God gave me came while I was sharing the gospel in simple situations. Quite recently, I met a former coworker. We worked together as teachers at Mackenzie High School in Guyana, South America, more than twenty years ago. This woman used to be an unsaved chain smoker, but now she is born-again and a pastor's wife. She said that over twenty years ago, I told her if God wanted her to smoke, he would have placed a chimney in her head. I cannot remember saying that to her. That statement affected her so much that she never forgot it. Now she is helping others stay free from that addiction. Thank God.

Occasionally, the Holy Spirit may impress on our hearts to share the message of the cross in some peculiar circumstances. In those situations, God will give us the courage and boldness we need. Getting started in a witnessing situation does call for courage and boldness, especially when one is alone. If we ask God to help us, he will. I have shared the gospel on planes, buses, subways, street corners, and trains. Friend, the Lord may need you as his special ambassador to get a message to someone who is in a once-in-a-lifetime peculiar situation, and you need to be up to the task. Consider Philip and the Ethiopian eunuch in Acts 8:26-40. God told Philip to leave a great revival and go to a lonely desert and explain the good news to a black Ethiopian financial minister on his way to Ethiopia.

Consider Ananias, who prayed for the Apostle Paul in Acts 9:10-19. Ananias tried to explain to God that Paul was not worthy of prayer, but God had a great plan for Paul's life. One day, I was preaching the gospel on a platform in the subway in New York City, and many people were passing by. Some might have thought that I was crazy, and, in fact, in a small way, I felt that way. Suddenly, a train came by, and when the door opened, a beautiful, well-dressed, Caucasian woman stepped out. With tears in her eyes, she came to me and said, "Preacher, please pray for me." I prayed for her the best I could, and she left. I am sure that in eternity God will make clear to me what happened that day.

You will receive many great inspirations while sharing the gospel of Christ. This may happen while you are doing so on a one-on-one basis or in group situations. It was during such exercises in the subway that the Lord inspired me to write two gospel fliers. The names of these fliers are "Joy in Heaven over One Sinner Who Repents" and "Jesus Paid for Your healing." As of this writing, I have printed over twenty-four thousand copies of these fliers. That number will continue to grow.

Try to find a common ground or point of reference, especially when sharing Christ with an individual. One morning, I was twenty seven-thousand feet high, flying in a Caribbean Airways jet, when I attempted to share Christ with the woman on my right. I began by commenting on what a beautiful day it was and how majestic the clouds were in the sky. I connected it to Christ by saying that it took much wisdom, knowledge, and power to create such a beautiful world. I suggested that God did it and explained how we can come to know him.

Be careful to keep the focus of your testimony and messages on Jesus and who he is. This message or good news is called the gospel of Jesus and ought to be shared with reference to his name and respect for his office as the Son of God. Isaiah 53:5 says, "But he was wounded for our transgressions, he was bruised for our iniquities: the chastisement of our peace was upon him: and with his stripes we are healed." The Apostle Paul said, "For I delivered unto you first of all that which also I received, how that Christ died for our sins according to the scriptures; And that he was buried, and that he rose again on the third day according to the scriptures: And that he was seen of Cephas, then of the twelve" (1 Corinthians 15:3-5). The Gospels give four detailed accounts of Christ's life on earth. Jesus is the God-man who came among us to redeem us; let us preach it, sing it, and shout it!

Satan always tries to entice us to behave in the wrong way to people who oppose us during the delivery of our message. If we get caught in his tricks, we will lose our focus. I listened admirably to a young man sharing the message of Christ to a group of people some years ago and thought of standing beside him to offer some encouragement and spiritual support. As I was contemplating making that move, one of the listeners made a negative comment about this young preacher. He reacted in anger by saying, "If you think you can do what I am doing, come and do it." His reaction was filled with such sharpness and anger that my admiration of this young man plummeted and it became difficult for me to support him. I knew he had lost his focus because of that distraction.

In a much greater way, many people, groups, and denominations have lost their focus on the message of Christ. One sure way to avoid being caught with many false groups, churches, denominations, and religions is by examining their focus. In 1 John 4:2-3, we see how we can test the correctness of the spirit of any religion or teaching by the way they focus on Christ. It says, "Hereby know we the spirit of God: Every spirit that confesseth that Jesus Christ is come in the flesh is of God: And every spirit that confesseth not that Jesus Christ is come in the flesh is not of God: and this is that spirit of antichrist, where of ye have heard that it should come; and even now already is in the world." To confess that Jesus Christ has come in the flesh is to say that he is the Son of God, who was born of a virgin, lived on the earth, suffered and died for our sins, was buried and arose again, and lives as Lord for evermore. I beg to repeat that our message needs to be based on this teaching.

In August of 1978, I was a student among a group of forty-eight people from my school who visited the Peoples Temple known as Jonestown, founded by Jim Jones, in the Northwest district of Guyana in South America. I was told by one of the teachers in our group that this was supposed to be the best example of a Christian Socialist community. To my amazement, they said nothing about Christ and his work during our visit there. Instead, I heard the dwellers in this commune praise Jim Jones, continually saying that he was a very good man and dear father who had saved them from many evils in the United States.

The emphasis placed on Jim Jones's goodness, with no reference to the person of Christ and his work, was very disturbing to me. To make it worst Jim Jones himself appeared suddenly, at the end of our tour, to make his speech, and he said nothing about Jesus. A few months later, the world was shocked by the news of the mass murder/suicide of about one thousand people in this commune. These people were forced to drink poisoned Kool-Aid by men pointing submachine guns at them, at the command of Jim Jones. Be on your guard; Satan can harm people in cults and religious groups whose beliefs are contrary to the teachings of Christ.

Being a faithful witness to our Lord and your local church is very important for your success as a Christian. Pastor Phillips Stephens of the Streams of Power Church of Trinidad and Tobago in the West Indies once said to me, "Most Christians like faith rather than faithfulness, and this is so because the word *faith* is associated with receiving (if ye have faith, ye shall have x, y, and z); faithfulness, however, requires that an individual remain steadfast and give even when it becomes difficult." Sharing Christ with others will become challenging sometimes, but faithfulness will keep you moving forward until victory is manifested.

Prayer is indispensible when sharing our Lord and Savior. It is through the working of the Holy Spirit as we pray that the hearts of sinners are made ready to receive the seed of God's word. I once heard Billy Graham, who is one of the greatest preachers ever, say, "The most important reason why I am successful as an evangelist is prayer; the second most important reason why I am successful as an evangelist is prayer; the third most important reason why I am successful as an evangelist is prayer. Every other thing comes after." He declared this to all of us, a gathering of evangelists, at the Conference of Evangelists, held in Amsterdam, the Netherlands, in the summer of 1986).

Sinners may reject the word of God when you share it, but never view such rejection as a failure. Do not take it personally. There are a multitude of reasons why people reject the word of God. Remember that it is by this exercise that we develop spiritual muscle. The more we share this message, the more the Lord strengthens us by anointing us to share him with more boldness and power. Your simple testimony of Christ's love makes you a great witness and an overcomer. Revelation 12:11 says, "And they overcame him (Satan) by the blood of the Lamb, and by the word of their testimony; and they loved not their lives unto the death."

We need to set Jesus's approach to evangelism as the gold standard for our evangelistic style. He never begged or pleaded with people to be saved but was commanding and positive. In Matthew 11:28, he says, "Come unto me, all ye that labor and are heavy laden and I will give you rest." In Luke 13:24, he said, "Strive to enter the straight gate: for many, I say unto you, will seek to enter and shall not be able." In the parable of the great supper (Luke 14:15-24) the Lord (who is Christ) commanded his servants to go into the highways and hedges, and compelled them to come in, that his house may be filled.

I was giving out fliers in Flatbush, New York, one day, when the Lord said to me, "Command the people to take the fliers." I hesitated to do so for a while, but when I started to do so, I got a better response. You see, my friend, in sharing the word of God, there are some people who are not willing to take it, and there are others who are willing but and hindered by the devil. We can help the second set of people to take the word of God by taking control over the devil through our command. It is time for the saints of God to arise and preach the good news of our Lord, Jesus Christ. In so doing, we will snatch men and women from the jaws of hell.

Supporting Scriptures on Witnessing:

"But sanctify the Lord God in your hearts: and be ready always to give an answer to every man that asked you a reason of the hope that is in you with meekness and fear" (1 Peter 3:15).

"The woman left her water pot, and went her way into the city, and said to the men, come see a man, which told me all things that ever I did: is not this the Christ?" (John 4:28-29).

"And He said unto them, Go ye into all the world, and preach the gospel to every creature . . . And they went forth, and preached everywhere, the Lord working with them, and confirming the word with signs following" (Mark 16:15, 20).

"The fruit of the righteous is a tree of life; and he that winneth souls is wise" (Proverbs 11:30).

NOTES

Desiring God's guidance in your life should not place you under an unreasonable burden. This guidance needs to develop out of a working relationship with your Lord.

CHAPTER 10

You're Not Alone, No, Never Alone

C hristians need to be conscious of the fact that the Lord is with, and guides them daily. There is the inner voice of the Holy Spirit that leads as well as instructs and directs us. And yet God is not limited in terms of what method he may use to guide us. For example, he may use a vision, a dream, our parents, a sermon from our pastor, a passage we read in the Bible, and any other way he may choose. It is our responsibility to pray so that sensitivity to his voice and leadership may develop in us.

The guidance of the Lord is very important if we are to be successful followers of Christ. The importance of the guidance of the Lord through the Holy Spirit (he is the Executive Officer of the Church) in the life of a believer can be compared to the importance of the navigational system of an aircraft. Without a navigational system, a plane is likely to have difficulty finding its destination and would be in danger of crashing. Without the Lord's guidance and presence, we will fail. Yes, we need to be led by the Lord daily.

Desiring God's guidance in your life should not place you under an unreasonable burden. This guidance needs to develop out of a working relationship with your Lord. Remember that as you make time for the Lord, you will discover that he has already made time for you. You are his priority. You are his sheep. In John 10:27-28, Jesus said, "My sheep hear my voice, and I know them, and they follow me: And I give them eternal life; and they shall never perish, neither shall any man pluck them out of my hand."

When God speaks, we need to respond. This may mean responding in prayer, helping someone in need, giving an offering, or in whatever way possible. Looking back on my life, I can see that my lack of response to God's direction is the major reason why I have failed many times. Please do not let that happen to you.

It is your God-given right to be led by his spirit, and your sensitivity to his voice will develop as you open your heart. Romans 8:14 says, "For as many as are led by the Spirit of God, they are the sons of God." Many people can miss God by expecting him to speak in a frightening voice thundering through the heavens, saying, "I am God. I want you to bow down and worship me." God, however, may choose to speak to us about worship by putting a longing in our heart for his presence. Further, the Lord may give you specific guidance about specific situations, but all that God tells you will line up with his word, which is the Bible. The word of God will shine much light on the way you live daily. It will do so as it corrects and instructs you. This is the first level of guidance. "Thy Word is a lamp unto my feet and a light unto my path" (Psalm 119:105). People who neglect simple instruction and teaching from the Bible and seek great spiritual guidance are on the road to deception.

I will never forget the dream I had of Jesus while I was in the home of Apostle Irma Gimith in Paramaribo, Suriname, in the early nineties. There was a longing in my heart to see Christ. I guess that desire was placed there at that particular moment by the Holy Spirit. In that dream, Jesus looked at me and said, "He that cometh after me, let him deny himself, and take up his cross, and follow me." Although these words are found in Matthew 16:24, Mark 8:34, and Luke 9:23, they came alive as Jesus spoke them to me. At times when I am tempted to doubt my calling, my heart remembers that moment. You see, to be told by Jesus to take up your cross and follow him is an invitation to continue where he left off; and we can be assured that he will never leave us as we make this journey.

As mentioned earlier in chapter 1, prayer is an important key to God's leading. The more we pray, the more we will be close to him and sensitive to his leadership. In our everyday life, the person who is closest to us is likely to be the one who knows more about us than anyone else, except in situations where we are hiding stuff from that person. God is not in the hiding business; he wants us to know him. How much time do you set apart every day to pray and read his word? The answer to this question should make clear your decision concerning how much of God's presence you will have.

In Matthew 28:20, Jesus said, "Lo, I am with you always, even to the end of the world." Friend, Jesus will keep his promise. The day you gave your heart to him, the eternal Holy Spirit of God came into your heart, and he will never leave you. God's plan for you extends throughout eternity. In John 3:16, we read, "For God so loved the world that he gave his only begotten son that whosoever believeth in him should not perish but have everlasting life." To put it simply, we have the connection to eternal life, which began the day we were born again.

Never forget that you are the other side of the bargain. Walking away from him can result in the loss of everything, including your soul. My pastor in Guyana, Pastor Basil Smart, often said, "Everything we do for God has two parts: God's part and our part; we cannot do God's part, and he will not do our part." Hebrews 2:3 says, "How shall we escape, if we neglect so great salvation; which at the first began to be spoken by the Lord, and was confirmed unto us by them that heard Him."

Remain faithful, and don't take your eyes off the prize; there are blessings (joy, peace, prosperity, fulfillment, health, and so much more) for you in this life, and when one thinks about eternity, as Brother Oral Roberts said, "it would be stunning." First Corinthians 2:9 reads, "But as it is written, eye hath not seen, nor ear heard, neither have entered into the heart of man, the things which God hath prepared for them that love Him."

As you continue to walk in the light which is Christ Jesus, God's richest blessings will continue to fall upon you.

NOTES

We need to know that prayer is an exercise that we can perform joyfully and that answered prayer will lead to ultimate joy.

CHAPTER 11

Five Life-Transforming Prayers

As mentioned early in this book, prayer is the divine privilege whereby we invite God into our life's circumstances. This became necessary because the human race walked away from God at the beginning of our history on this planet. The apostles asked our Lord Jesus to teach them how to pray, and this is very important because there are different types of prayer for different circumstances. The following are five types of prayer:

1. The prayer of repentance for the person who is beginning a relationship with God
2. The prayer of intercession by someone or a group of people who is standing in the gap, interceding or asking God's help on the behalf of others
3. The prayer of thanksgiving by someone or a group of people who is demonstrating an attitude of gratitude to God for all he has done
4. The prayer of faith, which is general in nature and can be used when desiring healing, deliverance, and other direct intervention we may need

5. The prayer for wisdom and revelation

Each type of prayer has a specific objective.

God has made himself obligated to answer prayers that are offered for the right reason and in the right way. Yes, I mean the right way. Even though God, in his mercy, may grant the request of a sinner, he is not obligated to answer the prayer of a sinner unless he first prays the prayer of repentance. Understand this clearly: we are all rebellious against God. This is so because we received a sinful nature from our fore-father Adam. Even though we may often receive help from God that we do not deserve, we will have to repent if we are going to have a lasting and meaningful relationship with him.

Many times, we pray out of great need or a burden from a particular situation, and that is acceptable to God, but we need to know that prayer is an exercise that can be performed joyfully, and that answered prayer will lead to ultimate joy. Imagine the most perilous situation in which you could find yourself: a cancer diagnosis or a great financial loss, for example. And then, through prayer, you are able to overcome it. This would bring great joy, wouldn't it? Again, imagine an unmarried person asking God for a life partner, after which the right person steps into their life. Wouldn't this occurrence joyfully commence a lifetime of happiness? Now we can understand why Jesus said, "Ask and ye shall receive, that your joy may be full" (John 16:24). There is no greater source of joy in the whole world than answered prayer.

The Prayer of Repentance

This prayer is for the enquirer, who may have read this book and does not know how to approach God in a prayer of repentance.

"Lord Jesus, I confess faith in your work on the cross. I thank you for all you did for me. You shed your blood on the cross; you descended into the regions of hell and the damned, where you defeated Satan and his evil workers; on the third day, you arose, demonstrating that you are the Son of God. You said if I will confess with my mouth that you are Lord and believe with my heart that God has raised you from the dead, I shall be saved (Romans 10:9). Lord Jesus, I confess that I am a sinner and ask you to please forgive my sin; I declare you as the Lord of my life and make a commitment to serve you for the rest of my days. Thank you for forgiving and cleansing me in your precious blood. I praise you for this in your wonderful name, dear Jesus. Amen."

"That if thou shall confess with thy mouth the Lord Jesus, and shall believe in thine heart that God has raised him from the dead, thou shall be saved" (Romans 10:9).

The Prayer of Intercession for a Lost Relative

Our unsaved relatives are very dear to us, and God promises that through our intercession, he will intervene and save those we love so dear. Yes, they may be in the company of terrible sinners, but God still promises to hear us when we pray. A great demonstration of this was Abraham's intercession for his nephew, Lot, in Genesis chapter 18. Even though Lot was surrounded by perversion and great evil in Sodom, God sent two angels and delivered him while Abraham was interceding.

In this age of the outpouring of the Holy Spirit, intercession by praying in the Spirit—that is, using your heavenly language—is very important when dealing with such cases. This is so because the Holy Spirit knows the complexity of people's situations and he can use us to pray them into deliverance when we are using the language of other tongues. This prayer should not cease until one sees the victory or has the witness in his heart that it is all right to stop. In some cases, you may have to take authority over the evil forces that are holding your loved ones in chains and break spiritual bondages before they can be set free. Always be very specific when you can.

"Father, I pray that the Holy Spirit, in his grace and mercy, will minister to___ (relative's name). Please do not look at his wrongdoings and disobedience to you and your word, but remember the blood of your son Jesus was shed to set him free. Dear Lord, I ask that you send someone in his path and allow circumstances in his life so that he will come to realize that he is lost and on the wrong road. In Jesus's name, on the authority of your word and because I am your child, I bind every demon, evil spirit, and messenger of Satan assigned to hold ___ (relative's name) captive, and I command them to loose ___ (relative's name) and let him go. Thank you for hearing and answering this prayer, Father. In Jesus's name, amen."

"But as for me and my house, we will serve the Lord" (Joshua 24:15).

The Prayer of Thanksgiving

One of the most beautiful prayers of thanksgiving was spoken by David, the king of Israel, in 2 Samuel 7:18-29. The occasion followed the response the Lord gave King David after he had thought of building a house for the Lord. The king had informed Nathan the prophet of his desire to build a house for God, and Nathan had told him that it was a very good idea. That night, however, the Lord appeared to Nathan and told him that he didn't want David to build him a house but rather Solomon, David's son, would build the house of the Lord. All David was requested to do was to prepare the materials for that house. God also told the prophet Nathan that he was going to do some additional mighty things for David. David became so overjoyed and thankful that he went before the Lord and offered a prayer of thanksgiving.

Please read the prayer of thanksgiving in 2 Samuel 7:18-29. If you make a personal prayer of thanksgiving to the Lord, it will bless your soul. Please let it be based on all the good things God has done for you.

"Wherefore, thou art great, O Lord God; for there is none like thee, neither is there any god beside thee. According to all that we have heard with our ears" (2 Samuel 7:22).

The Prayer for the Healing of Sickness and Disease

God can heal us in many ways, and the simplest is when we stand on his promises by believing what he said in the Bible. This blessing of healing is available to every believer. Yes, may I say, it is for all those who believe. Our God, the same God who forgives all our sins, will heal all our diseases. We see this in Psalm 103:1-3, especially verse 3, which say God forgives all our iniquities and heals all our diseases. There are numerous times when I have confessed his promises and received my healing in accordance with his word. People often ask, "Is it God's will to heal me?" In Matthew 8:3 and many other scriptures, Jesus declared that it is his will to heal. There is no place in the Bible where someone came to God/Jesus for healing and he said, "I can't. It is not my will to heal you," or, "Your time has passed."

The day you give your heart to Jesus, you became a child of God, and as a result, the children's bread, which is healing, is yours. The reason why Jesus is qualified to be our healer is because he paid the price for our healing when he took thirty-nine stripes on his back two thousand years ago. Forgiveness of sins and the healing of sicknesses and diseases were included in the same package, called salvation. Make sure you claim the whole package.

This is not an attempt to discredit doctors. I do believe that they are blessed by God to help us. God would not want anyone to suffer and die of a sickness simply because they refused to take a doctor's help. Remember to use wisdom in all that you do. At times, our faith may be tested with a stubborn sickness, disease, damaged organ, or difficulty. In those situations, you can hold your ground by confessing the word of God about being healed against all odds. It may take some time before your healing is manifested, but stay in faith until it happens.

It works according to your faith in God. The decision is yours to make. Use the doctor as much as you may choose, but remember that your faith can bring results in the most impossible situation. Sometimes a doctor's diagnosis can be wrong. In August of 2010, a doctor of a certain hospital told my sister that my mother had cancer in her womb and requested that we give written authorization for an operation. I told my sister we would not and would rather believe God in this situation. The doctor later changed his diagnosis and said that my mother had an infection and that it was treatable. I do not have all the answers for healing because God's methods of healing seem to be numerous. The Bible teaches us, however, that God will respond to our faith.

You will benefit greatly from memorizing some healing scriptures. They can be used as your first line of defense when sickness attacks you. The way to use them is to speak or confess them to yourself and others. Here are eight scriptures that I have memorized. Please take some time to read and memorize them: Psalm 103:1-3; Matthew 8:3, 7; Exodus 15:26; 1 Peter 2:24; 3 John 2; James 5:14-15; Mark 5:34; Isaiah 53:5.

I must add that some people do find it easy to receive their healing by faith because of their knowledge of the word of God, religious upbringing, experience, and teaching, whereas others might not. My suggestion to those who find receiving divine healing difficult is to get connected to a pastor, minister, or person who has knowledge and experience in this area and let them assist you. Please remember that it is salvation, which was made possible by the blood of Jesus, that makes one a child of God, and not one's belief in divine healing. In other words, we can choose not to believe in divine healing and still make it to heaven. Personally, however, I would rather have the benefit of divine healing and heaven.

A Prayer for Divine Healing

"Father, in Jesus's name, I thank you that your son Jesus took all my sickness and diseases when he received thirty-nine stripes on his back two thousand years ago. First Peter 2:24 says, 'Who his own self bore our sins on his own body on the tree that we, being dead to sins, should live unto righteousness: by whose stripes ye were healed.' Also in 3 John 2, your word says, 'Beloved (and we are the beloved) I wish above all things thou mayest prosper and be in health even as thy soul prospereth.' Lord, on the basis of these promises, I accept my healing and I thank you for restoring my health. I will continue to praise and bless your name as I look for the physical manifestation of perfect health in my body. In Jesus's name, amen."

This type of prayer you may need to say every day, several times a day, until perfect health is manifested.

"Who forgiveth all thine iniquities; who healeth all thy diseases" (Psalm 103:3).

The Prayer for Wisdom and Revelation

"Father, I ask for the spirit of wisdom and revelation in the knowledge of you: for the eyes of my understanding to be enlightened that I may know what the hope of your calling is and the riches of the glory of your inheritance in the saints. And what is the exceeding greatness of your power to me, who believes according to the working of your mighty power, which you wrought in Christ when you raised him from the dead and set him at your right hand in heavenly places. Far above all principality, and power, and might, and dominion, and every name that is named, not only in this world, but also in that which is to come."

"Father, I ask, in Jesus's name, that the quickening power of the Holy Spirit come alive in me. That you would grant me, according to the riches of your glory, to be strengthened with might by your Spirit in me. That Christ may dwell in my heart by faith; that being rooted and grounded in love, I may be able to comprehend, with all saints, what is the breadth, and length, and depth, and height; that I may know the love of Christ that passeth knowledge and be filled with all the fullness of God."

"Dear Lord Jesus, what will you have me to do? Please use me to be a blessing to others. May the seed of your word grow in me and bring forth fruit a hundredfold to the glory of your name. Amen!"

"If any of you lack wisdom, let him ask of God, that giveth to all men liberally, and upbraideth not; and it shall be given him" (James 1:5).

NOTES

NOTES

Some trials come suddenly upon us without warning,
but when we have invested time in meditation,
the beauty of God's word will flow out
of us in times of greatest need.

CHAPTER 12

Meditations from the Psalms and Epistles

Meditation is a time for private devotion, deeper reflection, and extended thinking on the word of God. When we devote time for reflection on the holy scriptures, the beauty of the Lord is revealed. This may be done by selecting a passage of scripture, for example Psalm 27, or by examining a number of verses on a topic.

In this section, I have selected five passages from the Holy Bible. Some of these scriptures have blessed billions of people, for a period, going back about three thousand years, from this time. Notable writers, such as Moses, King David, the Apostle Paul, and Disciple John, our Lord's brother, have penned many holy inspirations given to them by God. It is a few of these that I have incorporated into this book. How precious does Psalm 27:1 become when we are going through a time of trial and we read, "The Lord is my light and my salvation, whom shall I fear?"

Some trials come suddenly on us without warning, but when we have invested time in meditation, the beauty of God's word will flow out of us in times of greatest need. Yes, time spent on meditation will enrich us now and provide great strength in the future.

Meditation on the Psalms

The Psalms recorded in the scriptures were first used in ancient Israel to express praise and worship to God. They were sung or read in the temple or synagogue on Sabbath days and special occasions. These songs or hymns were usually accompanied by instruments, such as the harp and tambourine. Many of us can imagine the psalmist David as a shepherd sitting on the side of a mountain, watching over the sheep with his harp as he ministers; standing in the courts of King Saul, playing; or offering praises, adoration, and thanksgiving to God in the tabernacle.

It will be beneficial to approach the reading of the Psalms with reverence to God, and please invite the Holy Spirit to take these words from your heart to the throne of God. You may wonder how they were able to add music to the lyrics of many of the Psalms, but please remember that they were written in Hebrew. I heard one preacher jokingly say that they speak Hebrew in heaven.

Psalm 27

The Lord is my light and my salvation; whom shall I fear? The Lord is the strength of my life: of whom shall I be afraid?

When the wicked, even my enemies and my foes, came upon me to eat up my flesh, they stumbled and fell.

Though a host should encamp against me, my heart shall not fear: though war should rise against me, in this will I be confident.

One thing have I desired of the Lord, that will I seek after; that I may dwell in the house of the Lord all the days of my life, to behold the beauty of the Lord and to enquire in His temple.

For in the time of trouble He shall hide me in His pavilion: in the secret of His tabernacle shall He hide me; He shall set me up upon a rock.

And now shall mine head be lifted up above mine enemies round about me: therefore will I offer in His tabernacle sacrifices of joy: I will sing, yea, I will sing praises unto the Lord.

Hear, O Lord, when I cry with my voice: have mercy also upon me, and answer me.

When thou saidst, Seek ye my face; my heart said unto thee, Thy face, Lord, will I seek.

Hide not thy face far from me; put not thy servant away in anger: thou hast been my help; leave me not, neither forsake me, O God of my salvation.

When my father and my mother forsake me, then the Lord will take me up.

Teach me thy way, O Lord, and lead me in a plain path, because of mine enemies.

Deliver me not over unto the will of mine enemies: for false witnesses are risen up against me, and such as breathe out cruelty.

I had fainted, unless I had believed to see the goodness of the Lord in the Land of the living.

Wait on the Lord: be of good courage, and He shall strengthen thine heart: wait, I say, on the Lord.

Psalm 42

As the hart panteth after the water brooks, so panteth my soul after thee, O God.

My soul thirsteth for God, for the living God: when shall I come and appear before God?

My tears have been my meat day and night, while they continually say unto me, where is thy God?

When I remember these things, I pour out my soul in me. For I had gone with the multitude, I went with them to the house of God, with the voice of joy and praise, with a multitude that kept holyday.

Why art thou cast down, O my soul? And why art thou disquieted in me? Hope thou in God for I shall yet praise Him for the help of His countenance . . .

Yet the Lord will command His loving-kindness in the day time, and in the night his song shall be with me, and my prayer unto the God of my life.

I will say unto God my rock, why has thou forgotten me? Why go I mourning because of the oppression of the enemy?

As with a sword in my bones, mine enemies reproach me; while they say daily unto me, where is thy God?

Why art thou cast down, O my soul? why art thou disquieted within me? Hope thou in God: for I shall yet praise Him, who is the health of my countenance, and my God.

Meditations from the Epistles

Twenty-one of the twenty-seven books in the New Testament are called Epistles. An Epistle is a written message. These messages were written by the apostles, who, were inspired by the Holy Spirit to help the believers in Jesus Christ. Meditation on these Epistles enlightens us on the way we ought to live as New Testament believers and certainly makes clear instructions on how to walk victoriously in our Lord Jesus Christ. Indeed, spending much time in the Epistles is the key for building strong Christian character and living victoriously in Christ. To put it simply, the Epistles are there to show believers how to live from day to day in this evil world. The inspirations, corrections, admonitions, and illuminations that the first apostles and the Apostle Paul wrote to the early Christian believers are just as useful and up-to-date today as they were when they were written two thousand years ago.

Ephesians 5:1-14

Be ye therefore followers of God as dear children;

And walk in love, as Christ also hath loved us, and hath given Himself for us as an offering and a sacrifice to God for a sweet smelling savor.

But fornication and all uncleanness, or covetousness, let it not be once named among you, as becometh saints:

Neither filthiness, nor foolish talking, nor jesting which are not convenient, but rather giving of thanks.

For this ye know, that no whoremonger, nor unclean person, nor covetous man, who is an idolater hath any inheritance in the kingdom of Christ and of God.

Let no man deceive you with vain words: for because of these things cometh the wrath of God upon the children of disobedience.

Be ye not therefore partakers with them.

For ye were sometimes darkness, but now are ye light in the Lord: walk as children of light:

For the fruit of the Spirit is in all goodness and righteousness and truth;

Proving what is acceptable unto the Lord.

And have no fellowship with the unfruitful works of darkness, but rather reprove them.

For it is a shame, even to speak of those things which are done of them in secret.

But all things that are reproved are made manifest by the light: for whatsoever doth make manifest is light. Wherefore He saith, awake thou that sleepest, and arise from the dead and Christ shall give thee light.

Colossians 3:1-13

If ye then be risen with Christ, seek those things which are above, where Christ sitteth on the right hand of God.

Set your affection on things above, and not on the earth.

For ye are dead, and your life is hid with Christ in God.

When Christ, who is our life, shall appear, then shall ye also appear with Him in glory.

Mortify therefore your members which are upon the earth; fornication, uncleanness, inordinate affection, evil concupiscence, and covetousness which is idolatry. For which things' sake, the wrath of God cometh on the children of disobedience.

In the which ye also walked some time, when ye lived in them.

But now ye also put off all these; anger, wrath, malice, blasphemy, filthy communication out of your mouth.

Lie not one to another, seeing that ye have put off the old man with his deeds;

And have put on the new man, which is renewed in knowledge after the image of Him that created him.

Where there is neither Greek nor Jew, circumcision nor uncircumcision, Barbarian, Scythian, bond nor free: but Christ is all, and in all.

Put on therefore, as the elect of God, holy and beloved, bowels of mercies, kindness, humbleness of mind, meekness, longsuffering.

Forbearing one another, and forgiving one another, if any man has a quarrel against any; even as Christ forgave you, so also do ye.

1 John 4:1-11

Beloved, believe not every spirit, but try the spirits whether they are of God; because many false prophets are gone out into the world.

Hereby know you the Spirit of God: Every spirit that confesseth that Jesus Christ is come in the flesh is of God.

And every spirit that confesseth not that Jesus Christ is come in the flesh is not of God: and this is that spirit of antichrist, whereof ye have heard that it should come; and even now already it is in the world.

Ye are of God, little children, and have overcome them: because greater is He that is in you, than he that is in the world.

They are of the world: therefore speak they of the world, and the world heareth them.

We are of God: he that knoweth God heareth us; he that is not of God heareth not us. Hereby know we the spirit of truth, and the spirit of error.

Beloved, let us love one another: for love is of God; and everyone that loveth is born of God, and knoweth God.

He that loveth not knoweth not God: for God is loved.

In this was manifested the love of God towards us, because that God sent His only begotten Son into the world, that we might live through Him.

Herein is love, not that we loved God, but that He loved us, and sent His Son to be the propitiation for our sins.

Beloved, if God so loved us, we ought also to love one another.

NOTES

NOTES

The blessing of the Lord, it maketh rich,
and he addeth no sorrow with it.
Proverbs 10:22

The Power of the Blessing

Blessed! Yes, every believer is blessed, but most of us might not understand how important, or how powerful this blessing is. The blessing is the operation of the life of God in the daily lives of us, his saints, and in everything we do, so that we may prosper. Proverbs 10:22 says, "The blessing of the Lord, it maketh rich, and he addeth no sorrow with it." After God created mankind in the Garden of Eden, he gave him authority over all creation and blessed him. "And God blessed them, and God said unto them, be fruitful, and multiply, and replenish the earth, and subdue it: and have dominion over the fish of the sea and over the fowl of the air, and over every living thing that moveth on the earth" (Genesis 1:28). This blessing was necessary for mankind's prosperity or success. Without it, the power to progress spiritually and also naturally would have been absent. The earth that existed before man was created did not know this blessing until God released it.

After Adam sinned, the curse, which was brought about by sin, hindered the blessing from doing its work. We see the ground being barren, Cain killing Abel, Lamech killing a young man, and so on. A few people, such as Enoch and Noah, were able to reach out to God and receive elements of the blessing, but the full force of it was lost from creation. The curse became so great that violence and sin filled the earth, so God decided to rescue Noah and his family and destroy the earth with a flood. After the flood, God reinstated the blessing to Noah and his family. Genesis 9:1 reads, "And God Blessed Noah and his sons, and said unto them, be fruitful, and multiply, and replenish the earth." Yet the curse of sin was still operating on the earth because it required the sinless blood of the son of God to destroy it. God's plan was to send his son, Jesus Christ, to reinstate the fullness of the blessing.

To make a way for the son of God to appear, God establish a covenant of blessing with Abraham on the basis of his faith. Abraham validated this covenant with the sacrifice he made in Genesis chapters 15 and 22. Further, the blood of animals was used as a temporary provision for sin so that God's covenanted people, the children of Israel, might receive a conditional blessing.

Jesus made it possible for everyone, Jews and non Jews, to come under the fullness of the blessing when he died on the cross. This possibility becomes operational the moment we receive him (Christ) as our Lord and Savior. In spite of this, however, there are many Christians who do not understand what it is to be blessed by Christ Jesus and how to live under his blessing. It is the responsibility of the ministers of the gospel to teach this truth and declare the blessing of God on their flock.

Please remember that the very last thing Jesus did as he was leaving his disciples to go back to heaven was to bless them. Luke 24:50 and 51 says, "And he led them out as far as to Bethany, and he lifted up his hands, and blessed them. And it came to pass, that while he blessed them, he was parted from them, and carried up into heaven." This was not an artificial act but rather a necessary activity that released in them the power to prosper in all they did.

God does not curse his children or creation, and I do not enjoy making this illustration, but consider what would have happened to the disciples if Jesus had cursed them while he was being taken up to heaven. We will all agree that they would not have been able to do anything good. In reality, he blessed them and imparted to them the ability to prosper in all they did.

There is no silent blessing. The blessing is not released unless it is spoken or declared. It was spoken when God blessed Adam, Noah, Abraham, the disciples, and others. In Genesis 22:15-18, we read, "And the angel of the Lord called unto Abraham out of heaven the second time, and said, 'By myself have I sworn, saith the Lord, for because thou hast done this thing, and has not withheld thy son, thine only son: That in blessing I will bless thee, and in multiplying I will multiply thy seed as the stars of the heaven, and as the sand which is upon the seashore; and thy seed shall possess the gate of his enemies; and in thy seed shall all the nations of the earth be blessed.'" This was a very great blessing, and it was spoken.

Countries, economies, and governments that do not regard our Lord Jesus are under a curse and will come to a termination point, either by war, the transfer of power, economic failure, or some other means, unless a representative people from the populace in those societies become connected to the Lord God and invoke his blessing. In the fifth chapter of the book of Daniel is recorded the fall of Babylon, which was the world's most dominant empire. This destruction took place because they dishonored God. You may read Daniel chapters 2 and 5.

The United States owes its survival, from its time of infancy to this present era, to the blessing and favor of our Lord, Jesus Christ. Consider the battles that were won by George Washington when all the odds were against him and his army as they fought for independence, and the fact that we are presently the world's only super power and greatest food supplier after the Cold War has ended. We must not take this lightly, but rather, we must endeavor to keep God's word obeyed in these United States so that his favor might remain on us.

To the peoples, kingdoms, and governments of the world who have made Jesus Christ their Lord, the Prophet Isaiah declares in Isaiah 60:1-3, "Arise, shine, for thy light is come, and the glory of the Lord is risen upon thee. For, behold, the darkness shall cover the earth, and gross darkness the people: but the Lord shall arise upon thee, and his glory shall be seen upon thee. And the Gentiles shall come to thy light, and kings to the brightness of thy rising."

God told Moses to inform Aaron and the priests that it was their duty to release the blessing on the congregation of Israel. This was a formal blessing. Through Jesus Christ, we are incorporated into that blessing, which our spiritual Father Abraham received by faith. Galatians 3:13-14 says, "Christ hath redeemed us from the curse of the law, being made a curse for us: for it is written 'Cursed is everyone that hangeth on a tree; That the blessing of Abraham might come on the gentiles through Jesus Christ, that we might receive the promise of the Spirit through faith." Please do not forget that Jesus Christ, the son of God, is the author and finisher of the blessing and that he commanded us to declare it.

The Blessing

Please Receive the Blessing

And the Lord spake unto Moses, saying,

"Speak unto Aaron and unto his sons, saying, 'On this wise ye shall bless the children of Israel, saying unto them,

"The Lord bless thee, and keep thee:

The Lord make His face to shine upon thee, and be gracious unto thee:

The Lord lift up His countenance upon thee, and give thee peace."

And they shall put my name upon the children of Israel: and I will bless them.'"

Numbers 6:22-27

Blessed be the God and Father of our Lord Jesus Christ, who hath blessed us with all spiritual blessings in heavenly places in Christ.
Ephesians 1:3

And he (Jesus) led them out as far as Bethany, and lifted up his hands, and blessed them. And it came to pass, while he blessed them, he was parted from them, and carried up into heaven. And they worshiped him, and returned to Jerusalem with great joy: And were continually in the temple, praising and blessing God

Amen.
Luke 24:50-53

Kindly declare God's blessing on all people,
especially believers, as often as is possible and
appropriate; this will create an atmosphere for
faith, love, peace, and provision. I bless you in the
name of Jesus Christ, the Son of God!